Memory
Makers

OVER 100 ACTIVITIES
FOR GRANDPARENTS
and
THEIR GRANDCHILDREN

Written by:
Barbara Field and Marilyn Wheeler

Illustrated by:
Enola Porter

ACKNOWLEDGMENTS

The authors wish to thank:

Enola Porter for her clever illustrations.
Jeanne Field for her expert proofreading and editing skills.
Bill Wheeler for his support and encouragement.
Jason Wheeler for layout and design.

Their grandchildren:

Curtis	Eva	Makenna
Rachel F.	Samantha	Olivia
Nick	Christopher	Nate
Lucas	Sammy	Emma
Alex	Ellie	Grace
Matthew	Lauren	William
Rachel W.	Ben	Maia
Josh	Maggie	Cooper
Peyton	Lindsey	Quinn
		Ian

who made this book possible.

MAKING MEMORIES

The influence of grandparents on the lives of their grandchildren is immeasureable. Grandparents and grandchildren hold each other in a very special place in each others' hearts. It is a relationship like no other. Secret handshakes, private nicknames, made up games only your family plays, or special stuffed bedtime friends provide lifelong memories.

Grandparents not only bring a lifetime of experience to this relationship; they also bring patience and a willingness to slow down with children. Our bodies and our internal clocks move at a different pace and children seem to love that.

Children love simple games. Peek-a-boo with babies, hide-and-seek with toddlers, houses built under tables with preschoolers. Children may not remember these games, but they will hold the feeling of joy they had playing with you.

But as kids grow, their skills become more developed, and they become more action oriented. What do you do now? You'll find in this book plenty of things to do. You probably won't want to do them all, but try some things that are not normally a part of your comfort range. Don't be afraid if something doesn't work. You will be able to model the willingness to fail. You may actually learn some new skills for yourself.

Also, lots of projects have an acceptable outcome even if the product isn't perfect. The first sandwich a child makes may be misshapened, but it will taste especially good since he made it himself. If an art project turns out odd looking, so what? It's the process, not the product.

The activities in this book are not labeled for age levels. You'll know what your grandchild can do, what you are willing to try, and what to save until they are older. Have a great time trying these activities. Laugh, hug, sing.

So you are a grandparent. Lucky you!

TABLE OF CONTENTS

TABLE OF CONTENTS

WINTER

For families who live where there is a definite cold weather season, the pattern of daily life changes. As the temperature drops and people are primarily indoors, the pace of life is slower and quieter. So adults look for more intimate, cozy time with the kids. We have provided appealing activities for when the out of doors is frigid. Use this time with your grandkids for creative bonding together. Try these activities and add many more of your own.

JOURNAL KEEPING

For those grandparents who do not have the opportunity to see their grandchildren often, a journal is a good way to keep memories and watch children grow.

You may have materials for a journal already in your home. Use a standard-size 3-ring binder and fill it with a variety of papers. You can use unlined copy paper, wide-lined notebook paper, colored and white construction paper and even cardstock. Attach the child's picture and name on the cover of the notebook. Binders with a plastic insert on the front work well.

When your grandchildren visit your home, they can record their happy times at your house by drawing and/or writing about them. Let the children have access to a variety of pencils, pens, markers and crayons so they can choose what they like. If the child is not yet ready to write, let them dictate to you so they can record their memories. You can write on their drawings or on a following sheet. Remember to date each entry and to record each time they visit. Add photos if you wish.

What fun it will be to keep the memories. When the children are grown, you may have to debate who gets to keep the book.

TOY LENDING LIBRARY

If you like to keep your home orderly while your grandkids visit, try creating a toy library. First, collect the toys that are age appropriate for your visiting grandchildren. Then select an area in which to store them. For each child, make a library card with their name and picture and a way to record their checkout choices.

When visiting your house, let the children check out three items at a time from your library, or fewer if some toys require excessive space. Play the part of the librarian and explain the library rules. (Make yourself a library name badge if you like.) Children must return a toy before checking out a different one.

Children love this game, and you'll have more order in your home when they visit. What could be better?

Note: Don't forget to include books.

ART GALLERY

Somewhere in your home is a place to display your grandchildren's artwork. If the kids bring or send you their work, they are sharing something rare with you. You can support their creative efforts by showing their work off.

Look around for a special place in your kitchen, bedroom or recreation room where you can create a gallery. You might corkboard the area or simply use a removable adhesive to affix their works to the wall. You could even hang a clothesline in the laundry room and use clothespins to hold their papers.

A document frame from an office supply store creates a wonderful way to display unique pieces. Buy one that can easily be opened so artwork can be changed often. Be sure cousins have an opportunity to see each others' work displayed with equal importance. Collect some large flat boxes in which to save their best work when you change the gallery. Don't forget to have them date and sign their pieces.

If you have absolutely no other place for display, use your refrigerator and plenty of magnets. They will be proud to see their work in their grandparents' home.

LIL' PIGGY

Eating at a grandparent's home is a unique time to work on table manners with the kids. Here is a game to play that reinforces good habits.

First, discuss with the children the meaning of good manners at the dinner table. Let them help you make a list. Such as:

- elbows off the table
- chew and swallow food before talking
- only one person speaks at a time
- pass the food without reaching across another person or their plate
- ask to be excused before leaving the table

This list should reflect your families' values. Find or buy a stuffed pig (such as a Beanie Baby®) or small plastic pig to place in the center of the dinner table. Name her Lil' Piggy.

You play the game by having everyone watch during the meal for a person to break a rule. When a rule is broken, Lil' Piggy is passed to that person and placed beside their plate until someone else is caught using poor manners. Adults should occasionally break a rule to see if anyone catches them. Whoever has Lil' Piggy at the end of the meal must clear the table.

EASY CHEESY CORN SOUP

When the grandkids are tall enough and old enough to handle a can opener and a simmering pot, let them make soup. This basic soup is tasty and couldn't be easier.

Ingredients:

1 can	chicken broth
1 can	corn, drained
1 can	creamed corn
1/2 cup	small shell pasta
1/2 cup	shredded cheese or cubed processed cheese food

In a saucepan, place the broth, both cans of corn and the pasta. Simmer on stove until pasta is cooked, stirring occasionally. Add cheese and stir until melted. Season as desired.

See, wasn't that easy? Older kids can fix this and a sandwich for the younger kids.

Vary this any way you like. Add broccoli or chicken chunks. Try clams, shrimp, tuna or whatever strikes your fancy. Most kids will love this soup.

BREAD KNOTS

Do you have a grandchild that likes to tie things up? Well, put them to good use at dinnertime.

First, research some common knots and practice them with string or lightweight rope. (Grandpas are often a good source for knowing how to make knots.) Decide which ones you could use with bread dough. Then open a can of breadstick dough and separate into individual pieces. Using your hands, roll each stick into a 10"- to 12"- length resembling a rope. Carefully start twisting the dough into various knots and pinch the ends when a knot is complete. Place each knot on a greased cookie sheet and brush with an egg wash. Bake according to directions on dough can.

Note: Egg wash is made by mixing 1 Tbsp. water with 1 egg. Apply with a pastry brush.

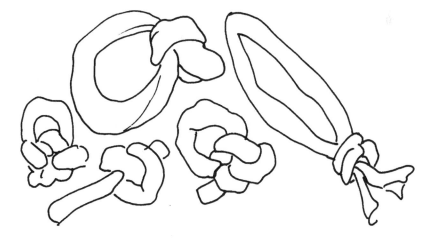

BROWNIES

What goes great with hot chocolate? Warm brownies. This very old recipe is simple and easy enough for little ones to help. Besides, what smells better than chocolate in the oven?

Ingredients:

1 cup	sugar
2 Tbsp.	cocoa (rounded) or 2 squares of semisweet chocolate
1/2 cup	melted margarine or butter
3	beaten eggs
1/2 cup	flour
1 tsp.	vanilla
1/2 cup	chopped pecans (optional)

Mix cocoa and sugar in medium bowl. Add melted butter or margarine. Then add the beaten eggs, flour, vanilla and nuts.

Bake in a greased pan for 30 minutes at 350°. Cut into squares while hot. For a single recipe, use an 8" x 8" pan, for a double recipe use a 10" x 12" pan.

Note: This recipe can easily be altered. You can frost the top while warm or cool, or you could add 1/2 cup of different flavorings, chips, or chunks of candy to the batter. Chocolate, mint or cinnamon chips work well. Experiment with it and have your grandkids choose and name the dessert after them.

HOT CHOCOLATE MIX

Let your grandchildren create a container of this dry mix to keep at your house for cold winter days.

Ingredients:

        An 8 quart-sized box of powdered milk
        2 pound box of instant cocoa mix
        6 ounce jar of nondairy creamer
        2/3 cup of powdered sugar

Mix well and store in a secure container. When ready to use, add 1/4 cup mixture to a cup of hot water. This is simple to make and great to drink after winter outdoor play.

FEED THE BIRDS

Naturalists tell us that birds do not need to be fed in wintertime. People do it to keep the birds in their yards so they can watch them. Keep a book identifying birds and a pair of binoculars handy. Make some simple birdfeeders and see what you can attract.

PINECONE FEEDER

Take your grandchild out on a pinecone hunt. Select the small to medium-sized cones. Try to find some that are not too mature. Bring them inside. Using string or wire, make a loop for hanging by wrapping around the top part of the cone. Spread peanut butter or solid vegetable shortening over the outside of the cone. (Don't try to fill the empty spaces.) Put some birdseed in a bag; drop the pinecone in and shake. The seed will adhere to the cone and you can hang your simple feeder outdoors where you can see it from your house.

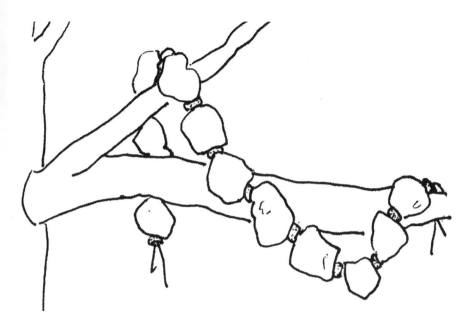

BAGEL FEEDER

Use day-old bagels and spread them with peanut butter or solid vegetable shortening. Drop the bagel into a bag of birdseed. Shake well and remove. Make a hanger by tying a loop of yarn through the bagel. Hang outside by the yarn loop.

GARLAND

If your grandchildren are old enough to handle a needle, try making a bird food garland. First, find a large needle with a blunt end such as a tapestry needle. Thread it with a medium-weight yarn. Cut cubes of stale bread and thread them on the yarn. You can alternate the bread with round dry breakfast cereal. Lay your garland over tree branches where birds will have access to it.

SASSY SALSA DIP

One evening when you have the older kids over for games and movies, let them make this simple dip.

Ingredients:

32 oz. pkg.	processed cheese food
16 oz. jar	salsa
10 1/2 oz. can	chili without beans

Cut the cheese into several small chunks and place in a crockpot with the salsa and chili. Stir and turn crockpot to high. Check and stir occasionally. When the mixture is nicely melted together, turn the temperature to low and keep the lid on. Serve with chips.

Note: You can use your microwave to make this dip. Just be aware of the individual unit's power level.

INDOOR OBSTACLE COURSE

When you have a round of bad weather and grandkids have pent-up energy, here's a lively activity for you. If you plan your space and set some clear guidelines, both the kids and you can have a lot of fun with an indoor obstacle course.

First, find an area in your home with space free of sharp edges or breakable items. Then look around for objects to set up 5 or 6 stations. You could find boxes, laundry baskets, hula hoops, 3- to 5-pound weights, large pillows or cushions, or an exercise ball. Now decide how to use these items and how the children should move to get to them. Figure out non-running movements such as skipping, 'baby' steps, walking sideways or backwards, crawling or slithering like a snake.

Lastly, plan how to move from station to station and what to do there. For example, skipping to the hula hoop and jumping in and out 5 times; walking to the cushions and doing 3 somersaults. It is a good idea to go through the whole course and show them what is expected before starting.

If you want, you can add music and a stopwatch to the event. Just remember, safety first.

> Note: A balance beam can be made by using a
> 2 x 4 placed on supports. Also, different-sized
> hardback books can be set up as hurdles
> to jump over.

INDOOR PICNIC

Do you have cabin fever? Are you and the grandkids anxious to be outdoors, but the weather won't permit it? Try having an indoor picnic instead.

Invite the kids to help you plan and create the scene. Would you like beach towels on the floor in front of the fireplace? You might dig out an old collection of seashells to arrange on your beach. Bathing suits make good attire. Bring some binoculars to 'spy' on the distant ocean.

What would you take to eat on a real picnic? Let the kids help pack bag lunches and drinks. You could put your food in a sand pail or backpack.

Don't forget to take along books, board games or other activities. (Better forget the Frisbee!) Just take along your biggest imagination and leave your worries 'at home'.

DANISH PANCAKES

Make these pancakes for a special breakfast or supper. Children like rolling them up.

Ingredients:

    2 eggs, whipped
    1 cup   milk
    1 cup   flour
    1 Tbsp.   sugar (optional)
    1 tsp.   salt

Using a mixer or blender, combine all ingredients and mix on low until well blended. Heat a large skillet to a medium heat. Spray with a cooking spray or melt a dollop of butter in center of pan. Pouring from the blender, lightly cover the bottom of the skillet to about 1 1/2 inches from the sides. This takes about 1/4 cup of batter. This makes very thin pancakes with uneven edges. When the edges are brown, carefully turn the pancakes over and cook the other side. Place on a plate and spread with a little butter and lightly sprinkle with additional sugar. Roll into a tube shape and eat while warm. This makes about ten large pancakes. Leftovers can be frozen. (Separate with waxed paper.)

Note: This is a basic crepe recipe and can be served with many kinds of filling. Omit sugar and fill the crepes with creamed chicken for a light supper. When used for breakfast, children like various fruit sauces poured on top.

SURPRISE CONES

Looking for something fun to make that's great fun to watch? Try your hand at making a surprise in an ice cream cone.

Place one sugar cone into a narrow fruit juice drinking glass, open end up. Put two tablespoons baking chips (chocolate, butterscotch, peanut butter, mint, etc.) into the bottom of the cone. Put in microwave 20 - 30 seconds. On top of the chips, place one regular-sized marshmallow.

Put the juice glass and cone into the microwave again for a few seconds. Recite some magic words (shazam, presto-chango, abracadabra, sesame rise, etc.) as the marshmallow puffs up. Remove from the microwave and eat when cool enough. Then make some more!

Note: For variety, heat a soft caramel for 10 -15 seconds before adding chips.

BUTTERSCOTCH GOODIES

These very easy cookies can be made by the youngest of your grandchildren.

Ingredients:

1/2 cup	peanut butter
8 oz.	butterscotch morsels
3 cups	crisp rice cereal

Melt chips and peanut butter in microwave or double boiler. Combine with cereal in a medium-sized bowl. Stir until cereal is coated. Grease an 8" x 8" pan.

Using a spatula or your hands, press the dough evenly into the pan. Chill until firm. Cut into wedges and serve.

Note: Try other flavors of chips such as cinnamon, mint or chocolate. Decorate the top with candies or sprinkles while still warm if desired.

CHINESE FORTUNE COOKIES

For the Chinese New Year or just for fun, try your little ones' hands at this treat.

Ingredients:

1	egg
1/4 cup	sugar
2 Tbsp.	corn oil
2 Tbsp.	water
1/3 cup	cornstarch

Beat egg with mixer until frothy. Slowly beat in sugar. Fold in corn oil. In a seperate bowl, blend cornstarch and water together.

Add cornstarch mixture to batter and mix. Spread tablespoons of batter, 4" apart, on a greased griddle at 350º. Cook until edges are lightly browned and cookies can be easily turned. Cook other side until brown.

Carefully handling the cookies while warm, fold in half, placing a written fortune in each one.

Bend in a 'C' shape and place each cookie in a muffin pan to hold shape while cooling. (Makes 12 cookies.)

*Note: Prepare your fortunes ahead of time using a
pencil and small-sized scraps of paper.
NO watercolor pens as they will bleed.*

PAPER SNOWFLAKES

Kids have been making paper snowflakes from the beginning of time. What a great tradition to continue! For very young kids, supply them with safety scissors and sturdy paper. Show them how to fold their paper in fourths and cut out pieces from the open edged corners.

Open up and see the surprise.

For older kids, tell them that snowflakes are really six-pointed crystals. The easiest way to make that kind of paper flake is to start with a circle. You can use a compass or items around the house from which to trace circles. Make several different sizes.

After cutting them out, fold each circle in half. Then fold into the center making equal thirds. Carefully cut designs into the corner point and along the sides. Open and display. Try different colors and weights of paper for different effects. Colored tissue paper is lovely.

Note: It's really interesting to pick out one room of your home and display so many flakes that it appears to be snowing indoors.

SNOWBALL GAME

Looking for something that could be used as a quiet indoor game? This simple activity is easy to do and fun to watch. Any age can play.

Take 10 to 20 cotton balls, 1 serving spoon, 1 container (such as a pie tin), and 1 blindfold. Seat the children on the floor in a circle. Sprinkle cotton balls on the floor in the center of the circle. Blindfold the first child after giving them the container and spoon.

If you have a large number of players, you will need to use a timer. Each player will try to pick up as many cotton balls as they can in the allotted time. No hands are allowed to touch the cotton balls. The player that has collected the most cotton balls could be the winner or just let each one have a try at it. It is lots of fun for the people watching.

CHEWING GUM RELAY

This is a fun, multigenerational, indoor game that requires dexterity, not running speed or strength.

You will need 2 pairs of thick winter gloves and 1 stick of gum for each player.

Divide your players into two teams. Place sticks of gum in a row in front of the players. The first player on each team puts on the gloves, picks up a stick of gum and unwraps his gum as quickly as possible. Then they take off the gloves and pass them to the next player. Each person on the team repeats the same process. The first team to complete the task is the winner.

Note: Small wrapped candies can be substituted for the gum.

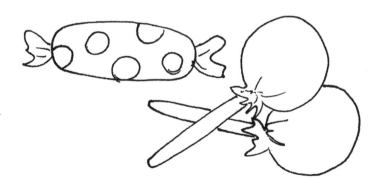

BEANARONI ART

This craft project is a good way to keep little hands busy when you have time-consuming chores.

Collect as many different shapes and colors of dried beans and macaroni as possible. You'll need a bottle of school or craft glue, craft sticks and paper plates.

Look around the house for some sturdy gluing surfaces. You might use a cardboard box, cereal box, Chinet® plates, etc. Choose a reasonable size since most of your pieces are small - 4" x 6" works well.

Use the paper plate to hold the glue, a little pile of beans, macaroni and the craft stick.

Have your grandkids use the craft stick to spread glue on the cardboard surface. They can make simple pictures or designs. See how creative they can be!

Note: Older children may want to plan a design first before adding beans and macaroni.

COLORFUL COFFEE FILTERS

This activity couldn't be more simple or fun. Many ages find this fascinating. You only need watercolor markers and paper coffee filters.

Cover your table and let each child have access to a variety of markers and a round filter. They should flatten the filter out and make simple lines, leaving some white areas. Intricate pictures and writing will not show up when completed.

When finished, place on cookie sheet and lightly spritz with a spray bottle filled with water. The process works best if the paper is damp and not wet. Watch the colors bleed into each other and create new colors. What happened to the lines?

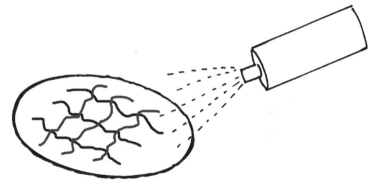

Allow to dry and iron if desired. If you wish, you could mount them on construction paper or hang them in a window as they have a stained-glass quality. After they are dried, a child might wish to make a picture or draw a design on their work. A sharp, fine-pointed, permanent black marker works great for that purpose.

PUDDING PAINTING

When you are in the mood to tolerate a mess, try this unusual painting activity. Kids love it.

Make up one box instant vanilla pudding. Place the pudding into 3 or 4 small containers. Add <u>powdered</u> or <u>gel</u> food coloring in each container. Primary colors are best. Insert a craft stick into each container. Provide aprons or painting shirts for each child. Many heavier-weight painting surfaces will work, such as poster board, brown paper bags, or card stock.

Have the children use craft sticks to put paint on the paper, but they should 'paint' with their fingers. Let them lick the paint from their fingers when changing colors.

Be sure to have plenty of wipes or paper towels handy. Cover floor surface if necessary. Let dry before displaying.

You can try painting too.

CINNAMON ORNAMENTS

Here is a truly unique way to make ornaments that can be saved for a long time. There are many variations of this recipe so work until you find a combination that you like. The basics are applesauce and cinnamon.

In a bowl, combine 3/4 to 1 cup of drained applesauce with a 1-oz. container of cinnamon. Mix together until pliable. Place the dough between two pieces of waxed paper. Press the dough flat until it is spread out enough to cut out with cookie cutters. Remove the top sheet of waxed paper and let dry until that side is no longer shiny. Turn over and let dry on the other side. Repeat if necessary. If desired, roll evenly with a rolling pin. Use cookie cutters to cut out any shape you wish. Hearts are especially nice for Valentine's Day.

Make a small hole for hanging the ornament. Something like a pencil or small straw will do. Your pieces will need to dry several days. Turn them over occasionally for faster drying. When dry, add a pretty ribbon for hanging.

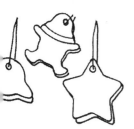

Note: If you wish, other ingredients may be added either for fragrance or to absorb more of the applesauce. Ground cloves or nutmeg, cocoa or even 2 Tbsp. of white glue are frequently used variations.

CRYSTALS

Are you in the mood for a long term project? One you and the grandkids are really willing to wait for the results? Grow some crystals. There are fancy expensive kits for sale, but you should start with what you have in the kitchen.

Materials:
a small, clean jar for each trial
pieces of cotton string
a short pencil for each trial
regular-sized paper clips
labeling material
sugar and salt

For each trial, cut and tie a piece of string to the center of each pencil. At the other end of the string, tie a paper clip for weight. The paper clip should be suspended into the cup.

Try making sugar crystals by mixing together 1 cup plus 2 Tbsp. of sugar with 1/2 cup hot water. Stir until dissolved. Pour into a clean, empty jar and then suspend the string down into the solution. The pencil should lie across the top of the jar. Label the jar "sugar". WAIT, WAIT, WAIT.

As the water slowly evaporates over many days, crystals will form along the string. Observe the shape of the crystals. Use a magnifying glass. Are all the shapes similar? This should be safe enough to eat.

Try the exact same procedure with table salt. Except use 3 Tbsp. of salt to 1/2 cup water. Remember to label the jar "salt". Do these crystals look like the sugar crystals?

If this is interesting to you and the grandkids, you might like to try the same amounts of Epsom salt, alum or baking soda.

You will still have to WAIT, WAIT, WAIT!

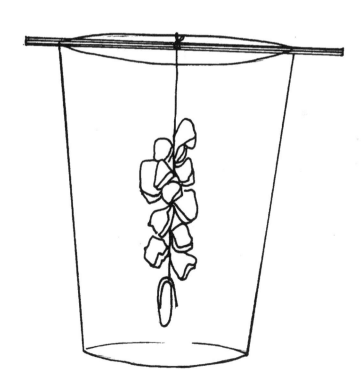

SPRING

When the grass turns green and the birds sing territorial songs, every human is ready to go outdoors. Tired of being locked inside, people need to be a part of a fresh, changing, colorful season as their own energy is renewed. Spring is a happy time and is reflected in the activities of Chapter Two.

BUTTERFLY SANDWICHES
(Open-faced)

Children of all ages love to make and eat these sandwiches.

Show each child how to cut one slice of bread into fourths diagonally. (A serrated plastic knife works well.) Let them spread peanut butter lightly on all four triangles and arrange the pieces in a butterfly shape. Place a mini carrot between the wings to represent the butterfly's body. Have the children decorate the wings with interesting edibles, such as round oat cereal, raisins and dried cranberries.

To add antennas, you can just insert Chinese noodles or pieces of licorice at the top of the sandwich.

Note: Cream cheese is a nice substitute for peanut butter. Square sandwich bread makes the best butterfly shape.

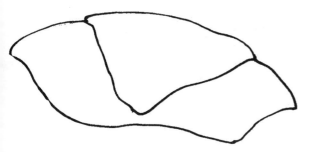

BREAKFAST COCOONS

This recipe is a very easy way to create a different breakfast treat.

You will need a can of commercial refrigerator crescent rolls . . . approximately two for each person served. Open the container and separate the triangular pieces. You can use your imagination about what to give your grandchildren to put inside the cocoon. They may wish to try marmalade, nuts, raisins, cinnamon chips, etc. or you can place small pieces of meat and cheese in the center of the dough and roll up from smallest to largest end of the triangle. Seal the ends together. Place on a cookie sheet and bake according to package directions. Serve warm.

Add a little fruit and milk, and you and the kids have made a complete breakfast.

Note: Commercial crescent rolls come in different sizes. The larger-sized rolls make the best cocoons.

HOW TO MAKE A SIMPLE SCARECROW

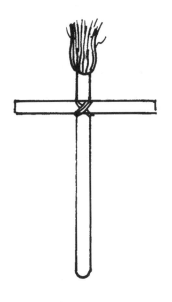

Do you have an old broom around the house? Let your grandkids turn it into a scarecrow for their garden.

First, find an old broom and stand it with the bristles up. Buy or cut a 4-foot length of 1" x 1" lumber. This becomes the arms. Measure down the broom handle about 6 inches and attach the arms as follows. If your grandkids are older, they can nail the two pieces together. Younger kids can use duct tape wrapped crisscrossed around the broom and lumber to attach the body together.

Then the fun begins here. Choose some old clothes that will be long enough to cover the body of the scarecrow. You could use an old long-sleeved shirt, dress or coat. Attach old gloves to the end of the arms with rubber bands, twist ties, or duct tape. Stuff if you desire, but it is not necessary.

Finally, create a simple face with 'found' items; maybe old sunglasses for eyes or cut pieces of empty plastic bottles for features. You'll want something that you can attach by pushing it into the bristles.

Find a soft spot in the garden and push the broom into the soil until it stands firmly in place. Watch to see if it scares birds away from your vegetables. If not, at least it should make you smile.

POP BOTTLE BIRDFEEDER

Here's a good opportunity to show your grandkids a way to reuse a disposable item. Plus, you can attract birds to your garden.

Materials:
1 plastic 2 liter bottle
a 5/16" dowel rod, cut 9" long
medium weight wire
drill or punch for hole making

Wash and completely dry the bottle. It will look better if you can remove the labels. Replace the lid. Turn the bottle upside down and poke or drill two small holes in the center of the bottom. Thread wire through one hole and out the other, leaving room to twist the ends together to make a loop for hanging. To avoid getting rain into the feeder, it is a good idea to seal the holes with hot glue, duct tape or caulking. (Wet seed will mold quickly.)

On opposite sides of the bottle, make holes large enough to put the dowel rod through the bottle so that it sticks out evenly on each side. Decide what kind of birds you want to feed. Merchants at a local seed store might be helpful with this. Then make a hole above the perch on each side where the bird can eat. Make sure the hole is the correct size for the food you select.

Fill your feeder (a funnel may help) and screw on the top. Try to find a location for hanging that is close enough to the house to see the birds feeding.

> *Note: If you would like to add more perches, just measure up about 3" and repeat the perch process.*

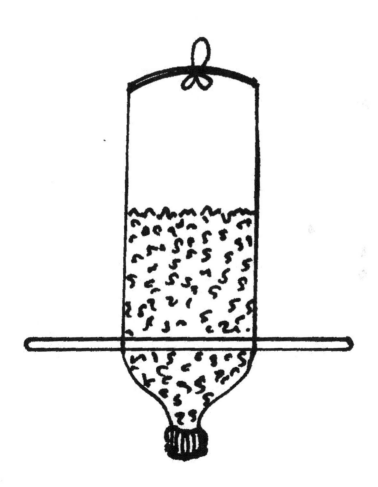

A FAIRY'S MAILBOX

People with imaginations have fairies living in their gardens. Do they live in yours? If so, give them a mailbox so they can send you messages.

Your mailbox can be as simple or elaborate as you choose. Look around the house for what you have that might work. It needs to be something that won't rust and has a door to easily open and close. An old mailbox or even just a plastic container will work. Be creative.

Fairies will write children thank-you notes when they tidy the garden, pull weeds or water plants. Sometimes fairies lose their wings and ask children for help in finding them. Feathers, flower petals, cicada wings or maple tree seed pods will work until new wings grow. Have the grandkids supply her with several choices and see which she prefers.

You can make fairies happiest by planting their favorite flowers . . . tulips, pansies, violets and pink hollyhocks. It is reported that garden fairies love to have children build them little homes from natural materials. See if the kids can find a quiet place near the mailbox to construct a simple home. Make a stick fence to mark the area. Then make little tables and chairs from nutshells or other found materials. Paint a few rocks for decoration. Sprinkling fairy dust (glitter) around the garden makes fairies very happy indeed. Grandparents with imagination can find multiple reasons to receive notes from garden fairies.

Also, listen very carefully at night as you fall asleep. On some nights you can hear fairy mothers sing while they rock their babies to sleep.

> Note: Watch for circles of fungi that appear during
> heavy rain periods. Legend has it that fairies
> love to gather at these circles to sing at nighttime.

RAISING CATERPILLARS

Children adore caterpillars. They love how caterpillars move and how they tickle when they crawl on your hand. The process of metamorphosis seems magical even to adults.

Unfortunately, many children have bad experiences raising caterpillars. The usual scenario is this: (1) the child finds a caterpillar (2) asks for permission to keep it (3) gets help making holes in a jar lid (4) runs outside for a handful of grass for food (5) two days later the caterpillar is dead. You may avoid this disaster by following these steps:

(1) allow your grandchild to only collect caterpillars that they have seen feeding on a leaf

(2) use only those leaves for food – caterpillars are very picky eaters

(3) put the food and caterpillar in a clean transparent deli-style container with a paper towel on the bottom

(4) keep out of direct sunlight and do not let condensation or mold build up inside the container

(5) clean the cage daily by removing waste and paper towel and add fresh leaves every day

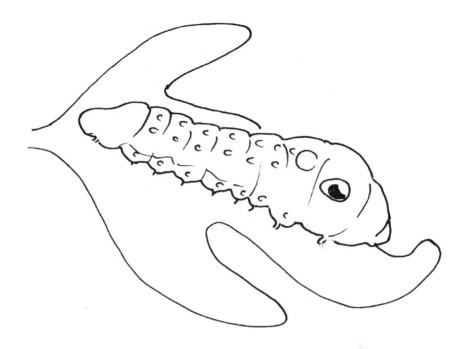

The time it takes until metamorphosis depends on the age and the species of your caterpillar. But when it is ready, it will pupate right in the cage. Throw away the excess food and waste. Now you wait and watch it daily.

If you have chosen a large enough cage, your butterfly or moth can hatch right there inside. The day before it hatches the pupa will change color and you can see the wings through its protective shell. Allow your butterfly 1 to 2 hours to dry before releasing.

A trip to the library will provide plenty of resource materials on butterflies and you may be able to determine just which butterfly or moth you raised. While you are waiting for the hatching, make yourself some "butterfly" sandwiches.

> Note: Caterpillars cannot hurt you as they have
> no teeth or stingers.

GRAMMY'S GARDEN

If you are lucky enough to have a home with some outdoor space and frequent access to your grandchildren, you have a wonderful opportunity to garden together. Your garden must be determined by your space, your interest and ability as well as the age and interest of the kids. Together you could fill one flower pot, grow an entire vegetable garden or try something in between.

If you are already a gardener, you know what to do. Start small. Find out what the kids would like to plant and see if that works for you.

If you are not already a gardener, the same advice holds . . . start small. There are plenty of places to go for help. Try a local university extension office. They are full of free advice and often have free written materials.

Select items that are easy to grow and that children enjoy. Seeds with quick germination rates are highly desired. In a vegetable garden, early peas and potatoes are fun; later, tomatoes from plant stock are nice, especially cherry varieties. Folks with plenty of room find that children love rows of corn and vines with pumpkins.

When it comes to flowers, zinnias are great. They germinate quickly and are not high maintenance. They now come in a very wide range of colors and styles.

Also old-fashioned morning glories and hollyhocks
have an appeal for children.

There is a lot of current interest in container
gardening. Many plants will grow on your porch or patio.
Just remember that container gardening requires more
watering than plants placed in the ground.

*Note: Do not put out more plants than you are willing
to care for. Kids have short attention spans.*

SONGBIRD NESTS

When birds first start to sing in the spring, look around for nesting activity. As you see some birds beginning to build their nests, try this edible version.

Ingredients:

1 stick	margarine
8 oz. pkg.	marshmallows
12	shredded wheat biscuits
1/2 cup	chocolate chips
1 pkg.	jelly bean eggs

Melt margarine, chocolate chips and marshmallows in pan or microwave. Stir. Crush shredded wheat biscuits in their bag with hands or rolling pin (Children love to do this). Add shredded wheat to the chocolate mixture.

Show your grandchild how to drop spoonfuls of mixture into cupcake papers placed in cupcake pans. Using a spoon, shape the mixture to look like a bird's nest. Cool. Add 3 jelly bean eggs to each nest.

Note: Your grandchild might like to tint small amounts of coconut with green food coloring to add to the nest before placing the eggs in it. Not necessary, but it looks and tastes good.

COMPOST PUDDING

If you've tried some gardening with the kids, explain what composting means or create a compost pile with them. After that, just for fun, make some compost pudding.

Ingredients:
    2 chocolate sandwich cookies per person
    3 oz. pkg.   chocolate instant pudding
    3 oz. pkg.   pistachio instant pudding
    4 cups   milk
    1 - 2   gummy worms per person

First, follow the directions on the pudding packages and make both flavors of pudding separately. Have the kids crush two cookies per person in a plastic bag. Choose clear cups or dessert bowls for each serving.

Lastly, create pudding cups by layering the puddings and the cookie crumbs. Try to get two layers of each. Let the kids hide a worm or two somewhere in the process. Chill and eat later with a smile.

BUG JUICE

Trick your grandkids into drinking a healthy beverage! Use a juicer, chopper or blender.

Ingredients:
- 1/2 bag (5 or 6 oz.) spinach leaves
- 1 or 2 apples, quartered
- 1 or 2 oranges, peeled and quartered
- 1 or 2 large carrots **or**
   - 10 or 12 baby carrots, peeled and cut up

Pour into a glass bottle and refrigerate. The liquid will settle into layers of different colors.

When your grandkids arrive at your house, tell them you have gathered some bugs from your yard for a new taste treat.

Stir the mixture and serve in 3 or 4-oz. cups. If they are brave enough to try the drink, reward them with a small treat. Then you can tell them the true ingredients or keep it a secret. They may ask for it the next time they come to your house, and you could even ask them to help you make it - a real challenge if they think the ingredients are truly bugs!

Note: This takes care of their fruit and veggie servings for one day. Make sure to remove the seeds from your apples and oranges.

BUGS IN A RUG

This old recipe is still great fun for young kids. Little children love to pretend they are eating real bugs.

Ingredients:
1 pkg.	6" flour tortillas (1 per person)
3 oz.	cream cheese, softened or whipped
1/4 cup	powdered sugar
1/4 tsp.	cinnamon
1/4 tsp.	vanilla
1/4 cup	raisins or Craisins
1/4 cup	chopped nuts

Mix together cream cheese, sugar, cinnamon and vanilla. Combine until smooth. Have your grandchild take 2 or 3 Tbsp. of this mixture and spread it on their tortilla. Sprinkle the raisins and chopped nuts evenly over the tortilla. Then have your grandchild roll it up. Roll each tortilla separately in plastic wrap and twist both ends tightly. Chill for one hour.

SPRING FLOWER BASKET

When the spring shrubs and bulbs are blooming, plan to have the grandkids take some flowers home with them. How about in a pretty homemade basket? You could make one as elaborate or as simple as you like.

Try this one. Purchase a piece of craft paper, 12" x 18", in a color that pleases each grandchild. From the shorter end measure off and trim a 1" strip to use for a handle. Take the remaining large piece and cut in half so that you have two pieces 9" x 11". Use a piece of scrap paper about that same size and cut out a heart shape. Practice with several pieces until you get a shape you like. (Folding the paper in half makes it easier.) When you've made a pattern you like, cut it out and trace around it on the paper in such a way as to create two identical pieces. Cut them out.

Then decide how to finish your baskets. You could use craft glue and apply to the inside of each piece along the side edges. Remember to glue the handle on at the same time.

An older child might prefer a more finished look. You may need to help with this. Using a hole punch, make holes along the edge about 1" apart with both pieces held tightly together. Then use a pretty cord or yarn and close the pieces together by whip stitching or using a running stitch. Remember to stitch on the handle. Then fill with flowers and have the grandkids take them home to Mom and Dad.

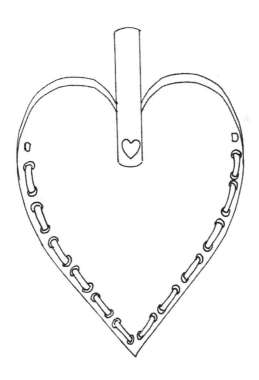

TISSUE PAPER FLOWERS

These simple flowers provide a lot of entertainment for not much money. Try making several and create a bouquet. You will need colored tissue paper or crepe paper and chenille stems. You can find these at a craft store.

Decide how large you want your flowers. It is possible to make them really large. You should probably start small. First, cut 8 paper rectangles - 5" x 7".

Along the 5" side, accordion fold all papers together. With scissors, round each end of the papers. Fold the papers in half. Then cut a small slit or notch on each side of the centerfold.

Fold your chenille stem in half and twist the chenille around the papers. Now twist the chenille tight enough to hold the papers together, but loose enough to separate the pieces. Then gently pull the layers of paper one at a time toward the middle of the flower. Arrange the paper until the flower seems carnation-like. Try multiple colors in a single flower. It looks pretty.

Note: The flower will look more finished if you take time to carefully separate each layer of paper by pulling towards the center.

CUPCAKE PAPER ART

If you've made some cupcakes for an Afternoon Tea, save a few of the papers for an easy art project.

Materials:
 A few cupcake liners of various colors
 A glue stick or craft glue
 Some scraps of colored construction paper
 Cardboard backing, paper plate, or sheet of construction paper

The shape of the cupcake liners resemble the shape of flowers. Let the kids use their imagination to create a single blossom for Mom, or a picture of a whole flower bed. Glue the bottom of the paper cup to whatever background you have. Use the colored paper scraps to make a decorative center. A little green paper for stems and leaves make a finished look. The smaller paper cups made for mini candies can be used for flower centers or tiny flowers by themselves.

Note: This is a good multi-age project. Older kids will just create a more mature product.

PAPER BEAD NECKLACES

This is fun for children with good hand coordination. They look so pretty even commercial artists create them.

Materials:
- a large 3 inch nail or pencil
- white school glue
- various kinds of paper such as: wrapping paper, classified ads, magazine pages, or construction paper
- stringing material such as: yarn, leather strips, heavy thread, twine, dental floss, elastic cord.

 Cut strips of paper in thin triangular shapes 6" to 8" long and 1/2" wide at one end and tapering to a point at the other end. Spread glue on the point of the paper strip with the base of the paper triangle flat against the nail, roll up the paper into a cylinder bead.

Glue the pointed end down to the rolled piece of paper and let dry. Make 15 to 20 beads per string.

Note: Try adding plastic or wooden beads or even seashells to the necklace. Use a sewing needle to string the beads.
These necklaces are 'keepers'.

EASY LEMON PIE

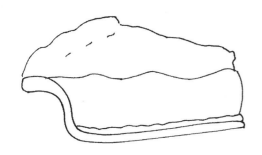

This recipe is so easy
that even the smallest
children can help,
and it's so tasty that
everyone will
want more.

Ingredients:

1 3/4 cups	milk
2 pkgs.	instant lemon pudding
6 oz. can	frozen lemonade concentrate, thawed
8 oz.	frozen whipped topping, defrosted
1	prepared crumb crust

Pour milk into a large bowl and add the instant pudding. Beat with mixer for 30 seconds. Add the thawed lemonade and beat for 30 seconds more. Carefully fold in the defrosted whipped topping. Spoon carefully into prepared crust. Refrigerate 4 hours.

Note: This is good enough for a special occasion dinner. You can use vanilla pudding in place of lemon or one of each.

AFTERNOON TEA

Who doesn't love a little 'spot' of tea in the afternoon? Little girls and boys do. Big girls and boys do. Sometimes even grumpy grandpas do.

Tea parties can be as fancy or plain as you want them to be. You can use little plastic children's dishes or your best china. You can often find inexpensive single cups at flea markets. A teapot for the beverage is fun. Matching is not required.

Use real tea if you wish, or substitute with apple juice, cider or lemonade. You'll also need a little something to eat. Store-bought fancy crackers or cookies will do, but it is fun to invite your 'guests' to cook. A butterfly sandwich is lovely; no-bake cookies are dandy; or make some little canapes.

Using cookie cutters, cut some shapes from sliced bread. Let the children spread the bread with butter, jam, peanut butter, cream cheese or whatever suits them. Serve.

What else can you do at a tea party? How about telling real family stories from the past? Could you each pretend to be someone famous and converse as if you were? Story times and sing-alongs are fun. Just pick out an activity your own family will enjoy and make plans to do it again.

PURPLE COWS

Make your grandkids laugh with this fun and refreshing drink. Simply add a scoop or two of vanilla ice cream to a 6 to 8 oz. glass and fill with grape soda. Add a straw. Enjoy!

> *Note: Little children do better with mini-servings (6 ounces or less). They also do better with the straws cut in half.*

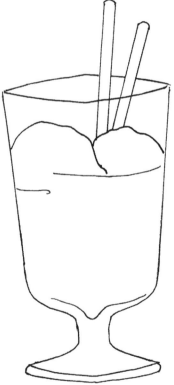

PEANUT BUTTER BALLS

Do the grandkids need an occasional treat?
Let them help make this simple four-ingredient snack.

Ingredients:
1/2 cup	chunky peanut butter
1/2 cup	confectioner's sugar
1 1/2 Tbsp.	margarine
3 squares	semi-sweet chocolate or 3 oz. chocolate chips

Mix together peanut butter and confectioner's sugar. Form into 1" balls. Melt chocolate and margarine together and stir, using a fork. Roll or dip the balls in the chocolate mixture and place on waxed paper. Store covered in the refrigerator. (Makes about 18 balls.)

KITCHEN XYLOPHONE

How about a little mood music while you're cooking in the kitchen? Let the grandkids create a musical octave with glass bottles, glass jars or water glasses, water and a metal spoon.

Since plastic is so prevalent in our culture at this time, it may be hard to collect seven glass containers that are the same size. You may need to solicit help from friends. When you have seven identical or similar glass containers, you can start to work. Measure up the side of each glass in 1/2" increments. Then have the kids pour water to the 1/2" mark in the first glass. Fill the second glass to the 1" mark; fill the third glass to the 1 1/2" mark, continuing to add 1/2" more water to each glass until you've filled all seven.

Place the glass containers in a row from least to greatest water amount. Gently tap each glass with the spoon and see what sound it makes.

Try tapping on different parts of the glass to see if you create different sounds on different places. Try a wooden or heavy plastic spoon for different sounds.

Now just tap around to your heart's content. Try some different rhythms. If you have a good ear and the notes seem a little 'off', try adding or subtracting water in each glass until you are happy with the sound.

If the kids have an interest, you might try making simple tunes in the key of C. Mark the glasses from C to B. Here's a tune to try: B,A,G…B,A,G…A,A,A,A,… G,G,G,G…B,A,G

Leaving the measurements on the side of the glass allows you to try this activity another day. Why not? You had to collect the bottles!

Note: It is not necessary to have identical glass, but it helps. People with a great sense of sound can make beautiful music with various water glasses. The thinner the glass, the prettier the sound.

TREASURE HUNTING

Who doesn't like to hunt for treasure? Everyone does, including little children. On occasion, when they come to visit, set up a treasure hunt. What good memories it will make.

Any hunt will have to be individually tailored to your grandkids' ages and their interests as well as your home. Where would be some fun hiding places?

Here is just a suggested list to get your ideas flowing:

On the front door place a sign that says:

TREASURE HUNT TODAY

See what treasure you can find by following the clues.

Clue 1 – Step inside and look under the entry rug.

Clue 2 – Now take giant steps to the piano bench and look inside.

Clue 3 – Next skip to your favorite doll and look in her hand.

Clue 4 – Hop on one foot to the largest plant in the house and look under the leaves.

Clue 5 – Take baby steps to the dining room
    and look under the chairs.

Clue 6 – Now walk backwards to the kitchen for the
    last clue. You'll find it in the fruit basket.

Clue 7 – Jump for joy all the way to the laundry
    room and open the dryer door!

Now what can the treasure prizes be? These, too,
must fit your situation. Here are some ideas:
    A new coin for a collection
    A paperback book
    An inexpensive toy
    Wrestling time with grandpa
    A craft project
    A rented video game or movie
    An invitation for a neighborhood walk
    A healthy treat waiting in the fridge
You get the idea. See what fun this can be!

Note: Other suggestions might be to have a Color
    or Alphabet Hunt for the younger ones.
    Clues for the Color Hunt will just have a clue
    with a color and they have to find the next
    one that is hidden on or under something of
    that color. For the Alphabet Hunt, you will
    hide the clues on, under or behind
    something that starts with the clue letter.

BEANIE BABY® ZOO

When you are 'rained in' and field trips are hard to do, set up a field trip in your own house. Ask the little ones to collect as many Beanie Babies®, stuffed animals, wooden animals, pictures, etc. as they can find. Gather these animals at your home. Tell them to make a pretend zoo all over your house. They can place animals under chairs, on tables, in boxes, on counters, near plants, wherever they choose. Arranging and rearranging is great fun. If they choose, cages can be created, but they know stuffed animals don't escape.

If there are older grandchildren with you when the zoo is built, let them make signage for each animal. It should include the animal's name and known information. If time and interest permits, further research could be done and added to the signage. The older child might also create zoo tickets for the trip to the zoo.

When the zoo is ready, create a pretend car with some chairs and 'drive' to your outing. Once they have arrived, you should be escorted around the whole zoo by the grandchildren with a commentary about the animals. Some animals may deserve a second look.

A nice way to finish the field trip would be with milk and animal crackers at a pretend concession stand.

FANCY PRETZEL RODS

You have no doubt seen packages of beautifully decorated pretzel rods. Well, you and your grandkids can make them for yourselves just as tasty and much cheaper. Just purchase a bag of 'giant' pretzels called rods. Look in your cupboard for melting chocolate, flavored chips, or caramel. Then look for decorating items. Do you have mini-candies, mini marshmallows, sprinkles, coconut, chopped nuts, or chocolate shavings? Be creative.

When you've gathered your materials, find a shallow platter or plate that will comfortably fit in your microwave. Melt an amount you can quickly work with. Lightly stir the melted base, hold the pretzels by one end and twirl until the top 2/3 is covered. Then sprinkle or roll the pretzel into decorative toppings to cover the base while it is still melted. Find sturdy glasses to stand the pretzels up until dry.

These are easy to make and eat and work well for parties, gatherings and picnics. You can color code them to the event . . . red and white for Valentine's Day; red, white and blue for the 4th of July, etc. Kids will love to show off their creations.

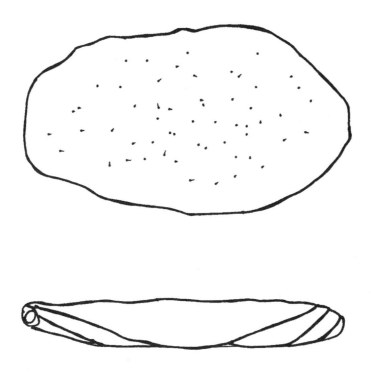

TORTILLA TREATS

For a simple snack, teach your grandkids to cook this Mexican treat. You will need small tortillas, margarine and cinnamon sugar.

Heat a griddle or frying pan to a medium temperature. Lightly spread margarine on one side of tortilla. Place in buttered frying pan until browned. Remove from pan and sprinkle cinnamon sugar on buttered side. Carefully roll in a tube and serve while warm.

Tasty and easy as can be!

SUMMER

Remember those 'lazy, hazy, crazy days of summer'? Well, that's when the kids are out of school and have lots of energy. Plan little vacations, field trips and plenty of water fun. This chapter has many outdoor activities, but also lots of quiet indoor times for recuperation.

NANA CAMP

If you have the time, energy and space, nothing is more rewarding than having a summer camp with your grandkids.

This activity demands lots of preplanning. It can be one day or one week long. Pick calendar dates months in advance so parents can save the days. You get to decide how many kids and what ages you can handle. If you have lots of grandkids, consider having a girls' camp and a boys' camp separately.

You may need help. You might want another adult at least part time, or assign an older grandchild as a camp counselor.

Everyone sleeps in sleeping bags in the room of your choice. Rules are given at the beginning and schedules can be posted each day so kids can see what is planned.

No baths at Nana Camp – just swimming each day, wading pools or sprinkler. Meals are planned ahead so little preparation is needed at mealtime. Quiet time each afternoon . . . lights out around 10:30 after a movie and a story read by Papa or an older child.

Days consist of crafts such as rock painting, going on hikes or to a museum, making potato necklaces, roller skating, having relays or watermelon seed spitting contests, obstacle courses, water gun fights, cooking, etc. Be flexible.

Have some options if it rains, or if an activity just 'bombs'. Plan a little evaluation time each day so you will know how things seem to be going for the kids.

Send them home happy, dirty and tired. Then you shower, pack a bag and head for a spa!

SUMMER PUNCH

This very simple recipe is right for summer days. Both children and adults enjoy it.

Decide how many servings you need. In a pitcher, let the children stir together equal amounts of lemonade and orange juice. Chill. Add ice to glasses when ready to serve. If you use this punch for a party, float orange and/ or lemon slices on top.

Note: You could also use this recipe for frozen ice pops.

STRAWBERRY BUBBLE-UP BAIT*

Get out your fishing poles and take your grandchildren fishing. Check your local conservation sites for locations or special fishing day events. Also, find out if anyone in your group needs a state fishing license before you go. Then make this easy bait:

1 1/4 cups	flour
1 1/2 cups	cornmeal
1 Tbsp.	sugar
1 tsp.	salt
1 oz.	box strawberry gelatin
1/2 cup	water

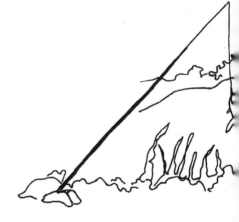

Mix together flour, cornmeal, sugar and salt. Boil 1/2 cup water. Add the gelatin to water and stir. Mix in dry ingredients. Let cool. Form into 1 inch balls.

Many children prefer this dough bait to live bait.

Note: A pair of inexpensive cotton gardening gloves makes it easier for a child to take a fish off the hook by themselves.

*This recipe was shared with us by the Missouri Dept. of Conservation.

NATURE TOURS

Take your grandchild on a nature tour. You won't need to travel to a special trail or to a center. You need only to leave your home. Your yard, garden or neighborhood will provide many things to discover.

Try some of these:
- Classify living and non-living things you find.
- Learn what kinds of rocks are in your garden.
- Examine different kinds of leaves for their colors and shapes. (Bring in some for rubbings.)
- Look under leaves for caterpillars.
- See if you can find flowers you didn't plant.
- Count the varieties of insects you can see.
- Are there mammals or evidence of mammals around?
- Listen for sounds of life.
- Dig small holes in various places. Does the dirt look the same?
- Lay a circle of string in the grass. Count how many living things you find inside the circle.

Start the activity when your grandkids are still in strollers. Just talk to them about what you see. As they grow, stretch their discoveries. When they are ready, have a nature scavenger hunt. This is a no-cost way of bonding with your grandkids as well as having a real learning experience.

PAINTING OUTDOORS

Many kids do not have enough opportunities to paint because it has the potential for considerable indoor mess. When spills happen outdoors, who cares? Just get the hose.

WATER ONLY

Let toddlers in on the activity. Just give them a bucket of water and a very big brush. They can just paint on anything they want, except people or animals. Let them brush stone walks, furniture, fences, trees, toys – whatever. Toddlers enjoy the act of brushing. They don't care if it disappears when dry. It will make you plenty happy though. Try this, it's fun!

MURAL MAKING

When the kids are a little older and can paint with tempera or watercolors, let them make an outdoor mural. Mix up some paints in cans with brushes. You won't need too many colors. Choose an outdoor place where drips or spills won't matter. Attach a long roll of paper or even newspaper want-ads (without pictures) to the side of a fence or other sturdy place. Provide old shirts or aprons to protect clothes. A temporary playhouse can be made from large appliance boxes which can be painted in their own fashion.

WATERCOLOR PICNIC

On a lovely spring day, pack a picnic lunch and watercolor supplies for everyone . . . you and Grandpa, too. Use your own yard or travel to a nearby park. While you are eating your lunches, look around for sights to paint. Make it simple . . . a tree, shrub, flower or garden sculpture. Whatever suits each person. While your pictures are drying, you can rest, read or play games. When back indoors, you can add your pictures to the Art Gallery, to the side of the refrigerator or the recycle bin.

Note: Take a keg of water for cleaning brushes.

"OUT" HOUSES

When the grandkids are older, they may want to paint a more lasting piece. If you or a friend has a detached garage, garden shed, tree house, doghouse or garden gate, you've got a potential painting spot. You'll need to provide some outdoor latex paints and good brushes. It works best if the adults and the kids agree on the design and colors. Planning the design first on paper and then chalking the outline on the surface of the building should create 'opportunities for discussion'. Less stress, happier folks.

SIDEWALK PAINT

Adapt this recipe for your situation . . . make a lot or a little as you desire.

> 1/2 cup   cornstarch
> 1/2 cup   water
> various colors of powdered or gel
> food coloring

Add cornstarch and water together in a container with a lid. Shake until cornstarch dissolves. Divide the mixture up by pouring into smaller jars with lids. Shake powdered food coloring into mixture and stir until you get the colors you want. Start with just a little and add more as needed to darken colors.

Rain or a garden hose will wash this artwork off. Great fun!

LUNCH ON A STICK

Use children's love of 'poking' things to create fun lunch kabobs. Bamboo skewers are available at many large supermarkets. You may wish to provide two sticks and let the children make both a protein-veggie stick and a fruit-dessert stick. Some kids might prefer to mix them up.

If you think your grandkids will take more than they can eat, just limit their choices. For very young children, you might break the skewer in half. If you just want a snack and not a full lunch, use toothpicks and fewer foods.

Use what you have at home, but these food possibilities will work:

Protein sticks might have ham cubes, cheese cubes, Little Smokies or hot dog pieces.

Veggie sticks could have mushrooms, olives, cherry tomatoes, pickles, broccoli spears, celery, snow peas.

Fruit sticks include
apple or banana
slices, kiwi, large
grapes, orange wedges, strawberries,
pineapple chunks.
Dessert sticks could be marshmallows, pound
or angel food cake cubes, brownie pieces.

Note: For the dessert sticks, a chocolate dip works great.

MELON BALL SALAD

Summer is the best fruit season and melons are a welcome addition to our summer menus. Even very little children can be shown how to use a melon baller to create a beautiful and delicious salad.

Use various melon types, such as watermelon, honeydew and cantaloupe. Cut wedges of the fruit large enough to make balls. Remove any seeds. Demonstrate to your grandchild how to use the melon baller. Make about equal number of balls of each fruit. Gently mix together and chill before serving. Add any little pieces of extra fruit to the bowl . . . no one will care if each piece of fruit is not a perfect ball.

SMOOTHIES

Smoothies are a good year-round treat, but they are especially nice in the summer heat. They are very flexible recipes and easily adapt to 'on hand' ingredients.

Choose 2 or 3 fresh or canned fruits, 1 flavor fruit juice and 1 flavor sherbet. Have the children place about equal amounts of each ingredient in a blender and blend until smooth. Serve immediately.

Experiment with different flavors and record the children's favorite combination.

A couple of simple ones to start with might be:

1 cup	pineapple chunks with juice
1 cup	sliced peaches with juice
1 cup	pineapple sherbet
1	banana, sliced

or

1 cup	frozen blueberries or strawberries
1 cup	orange juice
1	banana, sliced
6-8 oz.	plain or vanilla yogurt

Note: Choose different fruits and flavors of yogurt each time you make a smoothie and have the children guess what fruits are in it. Chilled glasses make this a special treat.

YANKEE NOODLE DANDIES

People love 'finger foods' at picnics. Let the grandkids help fix these simple cookies and watch them disappear.

Melt 12 oz. of chocolate chips with 12 oz. of butterscotch chips in a microwave or double boiler. Let the children quickly stir in two 3 oz. cans of Chinese noodles and 1/2 cup peanuts. Stir until all ingredients are coated. Show the kids how to drop by spoonfuls on waxed paper or coated cookie sheets. Keep chilled until ready to serve. (Makes 36 cookies)

CRUNCHY CHOCOLATE CANDY

Partially melt 12 oz. of semisweet chocolate chips in a double boiler or in a microwave. Stir until melted and smooth.

Have the grandkids crush 1 cup broken chocolate or vanilla sandwich cookies and a handful of chopped nuts to the melted chocolate.

Spoon into greased 8" x 8" square baking pan. Refrigerate.

BUBBLE FUN

Everyone loves bubbles. You can entertain a fussy toddler or a whole family reunion with magical soap bubbles.

Some grandmothers carry tiny bottles of bubble juice in their totes as instant fun for very little ones.

Bubble Juice Recipe:

> 4 oz.   good-quality liquid dish soap
> 32 oz. water

Mix together and let solution sit for several hours or overnight. You may want to add 1 or 2 oz. of glycerin (found in drug stores) to make bubbles strong. Humid, low-wind days are best for blowing bubbles as bubbles do not "pop" until a part of their surface dries out.

You can create many bubble tools from items you have at home. Look around. You'll find plastic rings that hold six-pack cans, plastic milk jugs with handles can be cut in half and some toys have handles with an open space.

To make really big bubbles, create a loop tool. Save the largest straws from fast food purchases. Cut <u>cotton</u> string and tie into a loop stringing 2 pieces of straws cut 4" long to form handles. Pull the string's knot inside one of the straw handles. Dip the loop into the 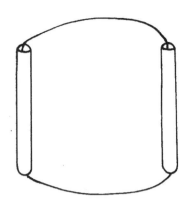 bubble juice until the string is saturated. Carefully holding the straw handles between the thumbs and index fingers, blow bubbles from the film made by the string.

Try making loop tools from different lengths of string. For little ones, try making a string 28 inches long. Experienced blowers can create gigantic bubbles with longer strings.

If you want to entertain at an outdoor party, place trays of bubble juice and tools on tables. Flat seed-starting trays work very well.

Note: Try to keep very little children from "swishing" the tools in the bubble juice. This action creates a scum of bubbles that can prevent bubble tools from forming a nice flat film of soap. Bubble juice can be reused. Avoid spilling on grass.

COW PATTIES

Here's an old-time favorite no-bake cookie that is easy enough for kids, and almost everyone likes. If the kids are old enough, let them make this recipe all by themselves.

Ingredients:

2 cups	sugar
3 Tbsp.	unsweetened cocoa powder
1 stick	margarine or butter
1/2 cup	milk
1 tsp.	vanilla extract
1/2 cup	peanut butter
3 cups	oatmeal

In a large saucepan, bring the sugar, cocoa, margarine and milk to a boil over medium heat. Remove from heat, add remaining ingredients and mix well until smooth. Cool for 5 minutes. Then drop by tablespoons on to waxed paper. Cool until set . . . usually one hour. Depending on the size, it makes about 3 dozen patties.

Note: You may want to add other ingredients, such as chopped nuts, coconut, chips or hard-coated candies.

EASY FRUIT PIZZA

Kids love to eat this simple pizza for lunch or afternoon snack.

Give each child a rice cake and provide a flavored cream cheese. Have them spread a heaping tablespoon of the cream cheese on the rice cake.

Provide 2 or 3 kinds of fresh or canned (drained) fruits for the children to place on the cream cheese. Use what you have available, but mandarin oranges, pineapple tidbits and dried cranberries are a tasty combination.

Eat immediately.

Note: Try different flavored rice cakes to see which your grandkids prefer.

THE AMAZING PARFAIT

The parfait has evolved over the years. It originally was a fancy, frozen layered dessert made with whipped cream and eggs cooked with syrup. Now it can be whatever you want it to be - breakfast, snack or dessert - and you can put whatever you want into the glass. It just needs to be layered and in a clear glass so the layers show.

Recipes can be found that use combinations of these ingredients: ice cream, sherbet, whipped cream, pudding, tapioca, yogurt, sour cream, jelly, cottage cheese, cake cubes, crumbled cookies, nuts, marshmallows, granola and fruits.

Which ingredients do your grandkids like? Let them layer some in a clear glass and chill. Abracadabra . . . parfait.

If you feel reluctant to experiment, here is a simple combination that works for breakfast. Alternate layers of vanilla yogurt, fresh strawberries, blueberries and raspberries. Add granola on top. What have you got? Three servings of fruit, one dairy, one grain, that's easy to make and good to eat. What else could you ask for?

FRUIT DIP

Summertime is so full of delicious fresh fruits that it seems people can hardly get enough of them. If you are having a special occasion, you can add this easy-to-make dip to enhance the fruit flavors.

Blend together one 8-oz. package of softened cream cheese and one 7-oz. jar of marshmallow cream. Using a mixer, blend until creamy. Chill.

Right before serving, help your grandchild cut various fruits into bite-sized pieces. Strawberries, kiwi, bananas, oranges, pears, peaches, grapes – whatever is fresh and available. Serve with party picks.

Everyone loves this.

BAGGED ICE CREAM

Looking for something unique to do that has a delicious outcome? It is hard to believe, but you can make ice cream in a plastic bag! Try it, it's fun.

In a small resealable plastic bag put:
      2 Tbsp.   sugar
      1 cup   half and half
      1/2 tsp.   vanilla flavoring

In a large resealable plastic bag put:
      1/2 cup   rock salt
      ice cubes to fill half the bag

Then put the small bag of ice cream mixture inside the large bag which contains both rock salt and ice cubes. Wrap a kitchen towel around the bag and shake it for 5 minutes. Remove the inner bag and use the towel to wipe off rock salt debris. Add any desired toppings and quickly eat. (Makes 2 servings)

Note: Try this outdoors as it is a messy project.

SUNDAE BARS

Nearly everyone likes to make their own sundae. Sundaes can be as simple or elaborate as you choose.

They require only three things :

      (1) ice cream
      (2) toppings
      (3) the opportunity to make them yourself.

Decide ahead of time how many people you will serve and how fancy you choose to be. This can be a party activity.

Let your grandchildren shop for this event if possible. Choose at least two flavors of ice cream and at least two toppings. You'll want plenty of sprinkles such

as chips, nuts, candies, coconut, etc. Aerosol whipped cream and cherries with their stems are great finishes.

Provide the dippers and bowls and get ready to party. You will know which children need guidance about amounts.

POTATO BEAD NECKLACES

If you have the patience for a time-consuming craft project, here is a great one.

Peel one or more potatoes and cut into small, irregular chunks about 1" x 1/2" thick. Make a hole completely through the middle of each chunk using a small nail, toothpick or ice pick. This needs to be done by adults or at least supervised by them.

Spread potato pieces on a cookie sheet or aluminum pan to dry for a day or two. Turn over occasionally. They do nicely if set out in the sun.

When completely dry, allow your child to paint each bead using small containers of acrylic craft paints and small paintbrushes. One or two colors are sufficient. Cover your painting area and supply a small container of water for cleaning brushes. The painting takes two or three sessions in order to paint all sides.

After all potato beads are dry, you are ready to string. Thread a large-eyed needle with heavy thread, cord or dental floss. Measure over each child's head to see how much cord is needed. Tie a knot in the end of the cord and start stringing.

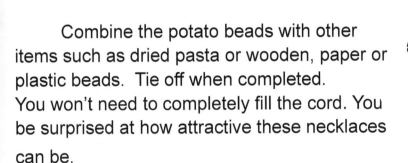

Combine the potato beads with other items such as dried pasta or wooden, paper or plastic beads. Tie off when completed.
You won't need to completely fill the cord. You be surprised at how attractive these necklaces can be.

> *Note: Acrylic hobby paints can be found at craft stores. Spray with polyurethane for permanent keeping.*

BEANBAG TOSS

This old-fashioned, multi-generational game is always fun. It can be part of your outdoor picnic games, or it can be adapted for indoor play. First, make some simple beanbags. Acquire some heavy-duty fabric and cut it into 2" x 3" rectangles or something similar. Fold in half and machine stitch two sides closed. Let the children help by filling the bags with beans. Then whipstitch the open side closed. Make at least six beanbags.

If you play toss indoors, find three baskets and mark off a throwing line. Just throw to see how many bags each person can get in the baskets.

When playing outdoors, create three concentric circles from ropes or hoops from other games. Create a bull's-eye target with the center being 1 foot in diameter, the second circle 2 ft. in diameter and the largest circle 3 ft. in diameter.

Establish a throwing line. Each player gets five bags at each turn and must keep one toe on the baseline when throwing. Assign points for each circle; such as 15, 10, 5, and take turns throwing, being sure each player has equal turns. The first player to reach 100 points wins, or make it a team effort and the first team to reach 100 points wins.

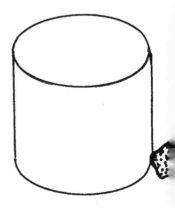

CONCENTRATION

There is no need to purchase a boxed set for this famous game. Just make your own.

Cut 2" x 3" cards from cardstock or construction paper. Find pictures with exact duplicates. You might use sheets of stickers, address labels, or magazine pictures. Glue or stick one picture to a paper card making sets of two identical cards. Create six or eight sets.

To play the game you and your grandkids should turn the cards upside down on the table and scramble them. The players take turns looking for a matching set by turning two cards over per play. If the cards do not match, they are turned back over and it is the next player's turn. If they match, the player keeps the cards and gets another turn. Continue until all cards are chosen. The person with the most cards wins.

Grandparents could create several sets of Concentration cards to vary the fun. Make more complex sets for older kids.

PICNIC FUN

Get the family together for at least one summer picnic. Let the grandkids help plan the menu and cook some of the food. Surprise everyone by playing 'old-fashioned' games.

SWEEPING RELAY GAME

Divide the 'picnickers' into two teams. Almost everyone can play. Provide a small rubber ball for each team and a broom. Create a starting and half-point line or split the team with players at both ends. Taking turns, each player on both teams must sweep, not hit, the ball to the halfway point or to the other half of the team without using their hands on the ball. The first team to finish wins. Create your own rules to fit your space and situation. Plastic eggs could be taped together with rocks inside them for a holiday relay.

WATER MARBLE PICK UP

Fill a large plastic tub or a child's wading pool with 6" to 10" of water. Divide your group into two teams, mixing up children and adults. Place chairs around the pool and toss in two dozen colorful marbles. Challenge the teams to pick up as many marbles using only their toes and no hands. The first team with 13 marbles wins. Who is better at this - children or adults?

Note: Adapt this game for the number of players.
Be sure to give everyone a turn.

WATERMELON TEETH

For a hysterical time, make false teeth for everyone at the picnic. It will definitely be a memorable event. After cutting the watermelon for dessert, use the rind. Cut off the green outer skin and the red pulp. From the white rind, cut a strip for each person measuring 1" to 1 1/2" wide and 3" to 4" long. It should be only about 1/8" thick. Using a sharp paring knife, cut a slit horizontally through the center of the piece, leaving 1/2" on each side. To form the teeth, cut slits 1/2" to 3/4" across the center cut. Be careful not to break the piece by cutting all the way to the top or bottom. Give false teeth to each person and instruct them to place them in their mouths in front of their own teeth. A group picture with big smiles will become a keepsake.

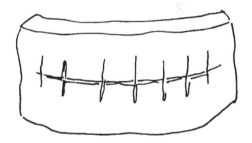

Note: Keep the false teeth in a plastic bag in a cooler if you are not using them right away.

WET SOCK RELAY

This is a great game for a hot summer day. Hang some twine or string for a clothesline between two trees, a fence or stakes in the ground. Use old (but clean) socks for the laundry. Gather up one clothespin for each sock needed and place in a container under the clothesline. Fill a bucket with water and submerge old socks. Mark a start line and position children behind it. The object of the game is to see how quickly the players can complete hanging the socks.

When they pull a sock out of the water, they should swing the sock around in a circle above their head 3 times before running to the line to hang the sock up. (This cools everyone off!) When all socks are hung up, reverse the process (one sock at a time) and finish with all clothespins and socks in their original places.

> *Note: Adapt this relay for any number of kids. Choose your number of socks according to the number of players, but you'll probably want each child to be able to hang at least two each.*

STOP, DROP AND READ

Be sure there is always plenty to read at your house when the grandkids come over. Your local librarians are enormously helpful in choosing books for different ages. When you get your own books . . . just pick up some for the kids.

But when they are reading or learning to read, have them remember to bring their own books with them. You'll love watching their reading progress.

Here's a family ritual that will stay in everyone's memory bank. Give this activity a family name if you want or just call it Stop, Drop and Read. Simply schedule a half hour in your day's plan for everyone in the house to read at the same time. You can use sofas, chairs, pillows, the floor . . . whatever suits you. But everyone reads.

How you plan this activity is up to you. Perhaps someone has a classic they would like to read aloud, or everyone can choose their own book. But everyone participates.

A little treat while reading is nice, but not necessary.

FALL

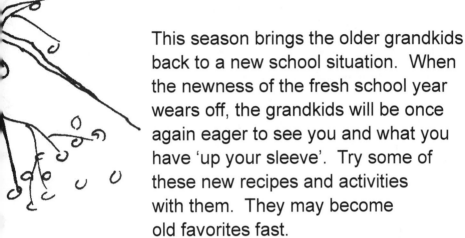

This season brings the older grandkids
back to a new school situation. When
the newness of the fresh school year
wears off, the grandkids will be once
again eager to see you and what you
have 'up your sleeve'. Try some of
these new recipes and activities
with them. They may become
old favorites fast.

AUTUMN LEAVES

Just about everyone loves the beautiful leaves of deciduous fall trees. A walk together in your neighborhood or local park can be a wonderful time to talk and pick up colorful leaves.

Bringing the leaves home doesn't have to be the end of the experience. You can save some as they are or use them for craft projects.

PRESERVING

A simple way to keep the leaves themselves is to iron them. Let your grandkids pick out the prettiest leaves. Place a piece of <u>waxed</u> paper (not <u>plastic wrap)</u> on the top and the bottom of each leaf. Let children who are old enough iron them with a low to medium hot iron on both sides. When the wax has cooled, gently remove the paper. The wax will keep the leaf from drying out and they should last several weeks.

Caution: A too hot iron will darken the colors of the leaf.

RUBBING

Use your leftover leaves to make interesting rubbings. Place leaves you want to make an outline of on a piece of paper; colored paper is nice. Peel paper from around broken crayons. Hold each leaf in place and using the side of a crayon, rub the outline of the leaf from its edges onto the paper. If you go completely around the leaf, you will see its image. Fill the paper with different leaf shapes and colors.

PRINTING

A final way to keep the memory of your leaf walk is to use the leaves for printing. Some inexpensive tempera paint can make beautiful prints. All ages enjoy this. Work with large sheets of paper. Supply a variety of paint colors. Lightly brush the paint on the top of each leaf. Place the leaf topside down on the paper and gently rub the back of the leaves. The color will transfer to the paper and preserve the image. Try multiple leaves and multiple colors. You may want to demonstrate this craft first for younger children so they see that only a small amount of paint is necessary.

Note: Prints make unique place mats for holiday tables. Office supply stores can laminate them.

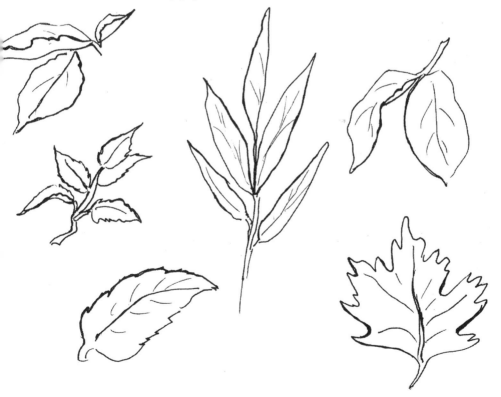

NATURE COLLAGE

How about a simple art project using found items from one of your nature walks? You might collect and bring inside such things as:

> leaves of different shapes
> small twigs   pinecones
> seed pods   dried flowers
> tree bark   small bones
> discarded insect exoskeletons
> (snakes, cicadas, etc.)
> small pebbles

Next, find some cardboard or similar material and cut to the desired size. Using a standard white glue, craft glue or rubber cement, completely coat the top side of the cardboard. Have your grandchild arrange his found pieces to please himself. It will be a reminder of your outing together.

Note: Leave songbird feathers and nests where they lay. It is against Federal Law to possess them.

SIMPLE APPLE BUTTER

Nearly everyone loves apple butter and here is an easy way to turn a long complicated process into a 'doable' project. Preheat a crockpot to its highest temperature.

Ingredients:

8 to 10	unwaxed cooking apples, washed, cored and cut into quarters
1 cup	apple cider or apple juice
1/4 cup	cider vinegar
1 cup	sugar
1/2 tsp.	ground cinnamon
1/8 tsp.	ground cloves
1/8 tsp.	ground allspice

Add all ingredients to crockpot. Cover and cook until tender, about 3 to 4 hrs. on High or 8 to 10 hrs. on Low. Stir occasionally. When apples are very soft, cool and carefully place in a blender or food processor. Puree. Spread on bread and enjoy.

Note: This activity nicely leads into apple crafts and the classic tale of Johnny Appleseed.

CIDER SLUSH

A warm fall day would be perfect for this simple treat that is a snap to make. For each person, use a freezer/microwavable cup. Have the kids fill the cup 3/4 full of cider. Cover and seal the top with plastic wrap and place in freezer. When ready to use, remove plastic wrap and place in microwave just until thawing begins. Watch through microwave window. Grab a spoon, stir it up and 'slurp' it down.

PUMPKIN SEEDS

At Halloween time, what do you do with the 'insides' of your pumpkins? Try washing the seeds and using them, sort of recycling. Dry the seeds and use them for mosaics or carefully string them for beads. Adventurous folks can roast and eat them. Here's how.

Collect and wash your seeds. Spread them on a nonstick cookie sheet. Spritz them with a cooking spray (butter flavor is nice). Let the kids sprinkle whatever seasoning they prefer on top of the seeds. Roast in the oven at 350° for 15 to 20 minutes. Stir two or three times while roasting. Remove from the oven, cool, and eat. Delicious.

PUMPKIN MUFFINS

These muffins are a great fall treat. They can be served for breakfast or even a Thanksgiving dinner. Have your grandchild notice the differences in the appearance and fragrances of the two spices.

Ingredients:

3 cups	sugar
1 cup	oil
1 tsp.	cinnamon
1 tsp.	nutmeg
1 tsp.	salt
4	eggs
2 cups	canned pumpkin
3 tsp.	baking soda
3 1/3 cups	flour
2/3 cup	water

Combine all ingredients in a large bowl using a mixer. Grease muffin pans or use muffin papers in baking pans. Fill cups 2/3 full. Bake at 350° for 20 minutes. (Makes 36 muffins.)

This recipe could also be used for making bread. It will make 3 small loaves or 2 large loaves of bread.

For the bread, bake at 350° for one hour.

CREATE YOUR OWN TRAIL MIX

Before you head outdoors for a nature tour or a walk, make some trail mix. It couldn't be simpler. See what your cabinets already contain.

Decide your choices and put out ingredients in bowls with spoons or measuring cups. You can either make individual bags for everyone or one large container. Use what you like, but be sure it is not all sugary.

Ingredients:
round oat cereal or
other cereals
nuts
dried fruits
pieces of beef jerky
small coated candy pieces
pretzels
sunflower seeds
Goldfish crackers

Mix together in a large bowl and stir. Enjoy in the out of doors or take along to public events where concession food is expensive.

FUDGE

With a little help, even the youngest children can make this delicious fudge.

Ingredients:
- 12 oz. pkg. semi-sweet chocolate chips
- 6 oz. pkg. butterscotch chips
- 1 can sweetened condensed milk
- 1 tsp. vanilla
- chopped nuts (optional)

Place all ingredients in a large microwavable bowl. Place in microwave and melt ingredients together. Stir until smooth. If desired, add chopped nuts here. Spray a 9"x 12" pan with cooking spray and spread mixture evenly in pan. Chill until firm. Using a table knife, help your grandchild cut it into bite-size pieces.

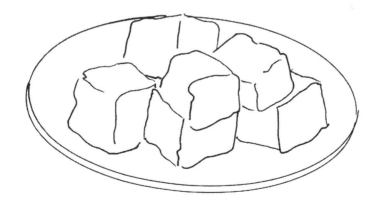

POWER BALLS

These little power dynamos are great healthy treats and easy to make.

Ingredients:

4 Tbsp.	wheat germ
4 Tbsp.	peanut butter
4 Tbsp.	powdered milk
1 1/2 Tbsp.	honey
	Sesame seeds

In a small bowl mix together all ingredients except sesame seeds. Roll mixture into 1" balls. Then roll in sesame seeds.

This recipe makes approximately 8 to 10 balls. Chill. Let your grandkids make these when they need an energy boost, some 'brain' food or just a tasty treat.

MUDDY POPCORN

When you have an 'overnight', treat your little guests to this indulgence. Mmmm, good!

Pop a desired amount of popcorn. In a microwave, melt 1/4 cup of stick margarine with 1/2 cup of chocolate chips. Mix well. Put the popcorn in a bowl and drizzle the chocolate mixture carefully over all the popcorn. Toss it with a wooden spoon or a spatula to cover all the kernels.

Eat this while warm, but provide plenty of napkins.

Note: Snow popcorn can be made by using white chocolate or almond bark instead of chocolate chips.

MOON ROCKS

Moon rocks are a nice treat to make before moon or stargazing.

Ingredients:
1/2 cup	peanut butter
1/2 cup	powdered milk
7 oz. jar	marshmallow creme (Kraft)
3/4 cup	dense, crunchy cereal

Mix all ingredients together and roll into 1" balls. Chill. This makes about 2 dozen balls.

While the balls are chilling, take your grandkids for a moonlight walk or to a planetarium. For older kids, consider renting an outer space science video.

Note: 'Health food' cereals that have large crispy pieces work well for this recipe.

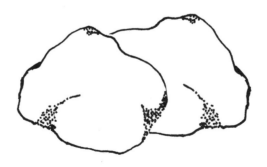

CARAMEL DIP

This is a quick and delicious dip that is great with sliced apples.

Ingredients:
30	caramels
1 to 2	Tbsp. water
1/4 cup + 2 Tbsp.	creamy or chunky peanut butter

Have your children unwrap caramels and place in a microwave safe bowl. Add water and microwave on high for 1 minute. Stir. Add peanut butter. Mix well. Microwave until smooth. (About 30 seconds.)

Note: Children like cutting apple slices with the gadget that slices and cores at the same time. You may need to help push and stabilize the apple.

PITA PIZZAS

Do you sometimes need to fix the kids a quick meal? Keep a few simple ingredients on the shelf and it's a snap.

Ingredients:

1	pkg. plain, whole, flat pitas (about 5)
2	cups shredded mozzarella cheese
1	jar pizza sauce
	Assorted toppings (pineapple chunks, black olives, peppers, onions, mushrooms, pepperoni slices, ham)
	Olive oil sprinkled with basil flakes (optional)

Brush olive oil unto both sides of each pita (optional). Sprinkle basil flakes onto both sides of each pita (optional). If you desire your bread a little crispy, place in a skillet and cook on each side for a few minutes.

Once they have cooled, have children spoon out about a tablespoon of pizza sauce onto each pita. Try not to spread the sauce all the way to the edge or it could get messy. Then children can add their toppings and shredded cheese. Let them experiment. They can make faces or designs with the toppings they choose. (Remember that the cheese will go on top and will cover their designs unless they want to put the cheese on first.) Make sure the toppings are spread evenly over the pita or they might not get warmed all the way through.

Bake the pizzas at 400° in a preheated oven for 5 to 10 minutes. Keep an eye on the cheese. When the cheese is melted and starting to brown, the pizzas are done.

RECYCLE BOX

What do you do on a cold fall day when everyone is indoors and out of sorts? Why go to the Recycle Box, of course. Find a large cardboard box or acquire a plastic bin. Fill it full of 'junk' you don't need but has creative potential in your grandkids' eyes. What could you collect?

egg cartons	small boxes
packing noodles	thread spools
foam packing pieces	small wood pieces
ribbons	empty paper tubes
fabrics	lids
buttons	plastic tabs
empty plastic bottles	clothes hangers

What can your kids do with your 'trash'? Can they create something useful? How about a game, a sculpture, or gifts for others? Some children can spend hours making something out of nothing.

FLUBBER

This amazing stuff seems to be both a solid and a liquid at the same time. It's irresistible to touch.

Ingredients:
>3 Tbsp.   water
>1 Tbsp.   white school glue
>2 - 3 Tbsp. Borax (a detergent booster)

Mix water with white school glue in a glass jar. Stir and mix well. If desired, add some food coloring. You need adult help at this point stirring in the Borax. Hands will be needed to manipulate the material. Remove from the jar and knead to make the material smooth.

What can you do with the results? How far will it stretch? How is it like a liquid?

If you store it in a sealed container, Flubber will last several weeks.

Note: If you find your Flubber too dry, add a little water; too soft, add more Borax.

KITCHEN BAND

Happy are the families where music seems to be a constant in their lives. Whistling while you work, singing rounds on car trips, instruments being tried out, songs at family gatherings. Music - every kind, everywhere. Even music in the kitchen with everyday utensils. Just see what fun you can occasionally have with a kitchen band where everyone gets to play. Try it – you may like it.

First, help the kids find a musical beat. Have them experiment and find a sound they like with wood, glass or metal kitchen items. Wooden spoons make good mallets or two together make clackers. Small plastic containers filled with a few beans or dry pasta make maracas. Bell sounds can come from a glass jar filled half full of water and tapped with a metal spoon. Empty oatmeal containers, tin canisters or a plastic bowl serve as drums. A wooden cutting board, a pot or pan, aluminum pie pans, or a metal grater – just tap and scrape to find new and interesting sounds.

When the percussion groups are ready, put on some music with a strong, steady beat and have them go at it. They might need a little direction on when and how they should play along. And the beat goes on.

> Note: If you and the kids really get into this, try adding a wash-board and thimbles. Washboards are not easy to find, but they make a wonderful sound and are nearly always used by real kitchen bands.

ORIGAMI CUP

Would you believe you could fold paper so that it will hold water? Well, you can and so can your grandkids if they are old enough to follow these directions and fold with some precision.

Start with a square sheet of paper.

1.  Valley fold in half, corner to corner.

2.  Fold right corner to meet opposite edge.

3.  Fold left corner to opposite corner.

4.  Fold down top corner. Repeat on back side.

5. Finished cup.

Squeeze the ends so a cup shape emerges. Then open up the middle and fill the cup with a small amount of water. Pour a gentle flow into the cup and drink quickly.

Note: Construction paper does not work, but copy or plain notebook paper will do.

PAPER HELICOPTER

Here's one that will entertain little ones and pique the curiosity of older children. Create a simple helicopter from paper and a paper clip and watch it fly.

Cut a strip of medium weight paper about 6 1/2" x 1 1/2". Fold in half. On one end, cut a 3" slit down the middle to the fold. That end makes the wings. Fold one half of the cut end down to the middle fold. Do the same with the other half except in the opposite direction.

On the piece of paper that is not cut and folded, attach an average sized paper clip to the bottom of the piece for weight. Just like that, you are ready to fly.

Take it outdoors and gently toss it up into the air and watch it glide down. It's fun to drop from a high place such as a window or tree branch.

Simple, old-fashioned fun!

Note: Some people believe that the paper flies better if it has been cut on the edges with decorative shears. Try it and see!

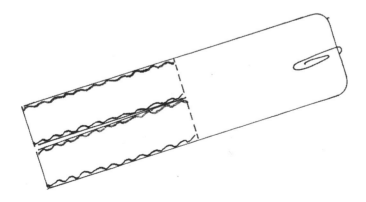

KITCHEN MAGIC

There is plenty of magic in kitchens. Sometimes you eat it, sometimes you don't. If you'd like to amaze the kids on occasion, try these simple tricks.

WATER WORKS

You need a small glass or cup (and a saucer to catch overflow). Ask your grandkids to fill the cup so full it won't hold any more water. Find an eye dropper or use a straw. Ask the kids to predict how many drops of water they think they can add until the cup overflows. Count as you drop the water in. Make sure no one jiggles the table or cup as you work. You'll be able to put many drops in before it overflows. Maybe 100 or 200. Careful observation shows that the water level is far above the rim of the cup before it runs over. It's kind of amazing.

Note: This, like all tricks, is not magic; it's just the nature of the surface tension of water.

THE SHARK AND LITTLE FISHES

This trick is lots of fun, but you have to be 'sneaky' with your finger.

You'll need a shallow pan such as a pie pan. Fill it half full of water. Give one of the grandkids a pepper shaker and ask them to liberally shake pepper into the pan. (Does it sink or float?) Tell the kids to pretend that the pepper flakes are little tiny fishes.

Now, here's the trick. Somehow (out of view) find a way to apply a little soap on your index finger. Then say that your finger has become a shark. Put your finger in the middle of the peppered water and watch all the little fish move away. This is so much fun that you can give the trick away and let the kids try it. They'll want to do it over and over.

DANCING RAISINS

Got a few raisins in your cupboard? Try this: Take 2 clear small glasses. Fill one with 2" of tap water. Drop 4 to 6 raisins in the water. Do they sink or float? Now put 2" of clear, carbonated soda in the other glass and add the same number of raisins to this glass. What happens to the raisins in the glass? Do they sink, float or dance? If you don't mind a little 'white lie', tell the kids the sugar in the soda makes the raisins hyper. Why DO the raisins bob up and down?

Note: When the 'dancing' slows down, swirl the glass slightly to see if the raisins revive.

MAGIC PUDDING

This is fun to try around St. Patrick's Day.
Pour the contents of a box of instant Pistachio pudding into another container so you can't tell what it is. Have each grandchild put 4 oz. of milk into a small container with a lid, such as a baby food jar.

Then have each grandchild put a tablespoonful of the 'magic' powder into the container and fasten the lid. Ask the kids to shake it up. What happened to this mixture? Let it sit for a bit and presto . . . magic pudding.

EDIBLE PLAY DOUGH

If your family still has toddlers who like to put objects in their mouths, here's a project for you. Dough they can mold and eat. What more could a toddler want?

You need:
  1 18 oz. jar creamy peanut butter
  6 Tbsp.   honey
  3/4 cup   nonfat dry milk (approx.)

In a medium-sized bowl, mix together peanut butter and honey. Slowly add dry milk to mixture. This will not be an exact amount. Knead with your fingers until it has a workable dough texture.

Carefully wash little hands. Give each child a cookie sheet, a plastic knife (not serrated) and a few decorations in a cup. Decorations could be small candies, round dry cereal, raisins or Craisins . . . whatever edible items you have at home. Give them a 'gob' of dough and let them mold it to their hearts' content. They might be willing to save a sculpture or two for dessert, but probably not.

Note: If the dough gets too sticky while being worked, just add more powdered milk.

PLACE MATS

When fall holidays approach, children like to contribute to the festivities. One way to do it is to make simple place mats. An easy method for younger kids is to give them 12" x 8" art papers that they can draw on. You can take the best ones to a local office supply store and have them laminated. They will last quite a while, and it will please the kids when their place mats are used on the table.

A second method for older children is to use cloth. Purchase some heavyweight, washable cotton (even canvas will do). Cut as many 12" x 8" pieces as you need. The side edges can be finished by hand stitch or by machine, but raveling makes a pretty edge.

On to decorating! You'll need a few colors of fabric paint or fabric markers from a craft store. Let the kids decide if they want to paint or print a design on the fabric. Decorating the corners of the place mats work best as the design can still be seen when a plate is added to the mat.

If the kids haven't done any printing, encourage that choice. When you make Simple Apple Butter, save an apple or two, cut in half and using a brush, carefully coat it with fabric paint. Practice on scraps before printing on the prepared place mats. Potatoes are good print makers too. Use the same process as the apple prints. Printing has endless possibilities. Try several of them.

PILLOW PALS

This is a lovely way to spend an afternoon. Let your grandkids make a snuggly pillow for their pet, stuffed animal or themselves. Find some fabric that is soft and does not ravel.

Decide what shape and size pillow to make. Cut the fabric out, put together with right sides facing each other. Use a pencil and a ruler to draw lines to stitch along on the wrong (outside) of the pillow. Secure the two sides with extra long straight pins with the knobbed heads as these are easier for children to manage.

Teach your grandchild how to thread a needle and knot the thread. Show them the basic running stitch. Leave one side open for filling. Use some sort of washable filling, such as polyfiber fill and stuff the pillow to desired fullness.

Teach your grandchild the slipstitch to close the opening.

Make one for yourself and take a good nap.

POTATO PEOPLE

Keep your grandkids engaged while you're cooking a big dinner. Try keeping them busy creating people from potatoes. These can be your table centerpiece.

Use Idaho potatoes and decide which part of the potato will be the face. Help the kids cut off the bottom end so the potato will stand up alone. Provide them with plenty of food items for features on the head. For example: baby carrots, raisins, miniature marshmallows, string beans, mushrooms, uncooked spaghetti, Chinese noodles, olives or peanuts in the shell. Attach these items with straight pins or pieces of round toothpicks.

Have the children name their character and create a story about him or her.

Note: Smaller children will likely need some assistance attaching food items. Make a small hole with a toothpick in the potato before attaching spaghetti.

ROCKIN' ART

Archeologists know that the earliest form of graphic communication was the rock paintings cavemen placed on the walls of their cave homes. People have never stopped painting rocks. It's inexpensive to do and a joy to create.

This activity is great for beginning and advanced artists. Rocks can be found in arts and craft stores, landscape and lumber suppliers, near rivers or lakes, parks or maybe in your own yard.

Materials needed are:
- acrylic paints (white, black, blue, red, yellow)
- paper plates
- brushes of different sizes
- cups of water to clean brushes
- paper towels
- newspaper to protect work area
- soft lead pencils
- scraps of paper
- round toothpicks
- small pieces of sponge
- thin-lined black permanent marker for outlining after dry (optional)

Start with clean rocks. Scrub them with water and dish detergent. Then dry them out in the sun for a day or two before painting.

Ask the children to study the shape of their rocks and decide what they might resemble: food, pets, a baseball, football, volcano, flowers, car, etc.

Each child should choose two rocks – one to paint on while the other is drying. Ask them to sketch some designs on paper first, and then on the rock with the soft pencil.

Use only a small amount of the colors they want on the paper plate palette to begin with. Besides brushing they might want to dab on paint with a sponge, or make dots with the toothpicks.

Painted rocks make great paperweights, doorstops, bookends, or garden decorations.

Masterpieces to behold!

Note: *If you wish to protect the completed rock,*
give it a coat of acrylic sealer after it is
completely dry.

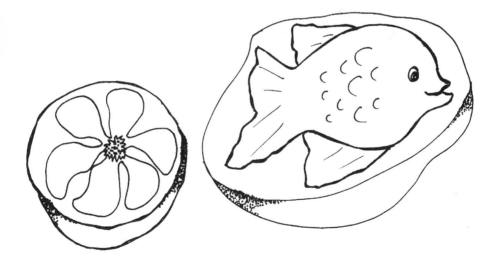

INDEX

Marilyn and Barbara live in the greater Kansas City area - one on each side of the Kansas/Missouri border.

Together they have taught for over 40 years, and combined they have 28 grandchildren. This book was a "natural" for them.

Made in the USA
Charleston, SC
15 June 2012